My Green Lunch

Colleen Hord

ROURKE PUBLISHING
www.rourkepublishing.com

www.rourkepublishing.com

PHOTO CREDITS: Cover, Page 15: © Ivonne Wierink; Title Page, Page 4, 21: © Cathy Yeulet; Page 5: © Igor Dutina; Page 7: © Gary Cookson; Page 8: © William Berry; Page 10: © Dmitry Ternovoy; Page 11: © Shannon Long; Page 12: © Ebolyukh; Page 13: © Zhannaprokopeva; Page 15: © Glenda Powers; Page 17 :© Mike Flippo; Page 18: © Stephanie DeLay; Page 19: © Chris Price; Page 9: © 4774344sean

Edited by Kelli L. Hicks

Cover and Interior design by Tara Raymo

Library of Congress Cataloging-in-Publication Data

Hord, Colleen.
 My green lunch / Colleen Hord.
    p. cm. -- (Green earth science)
 Includes bibliographical references and index.
 ISBN 978-1-61590-302-3 (Hard Cover) (alk. paper)
 ISBN 978-1-61590-541-6 (Soft Cover)
 1. Food--Environmental aspects--Juvenile literature. I. Title.
 TX355.H57 2011
 178--dc22
                              2010009641

Rourke Publishing
Printed in the United States of America, North Mankato, Minnesota
020111
01312011LP-A

www.rourkepublishing.com - rourke@rourkepublishing.com
Post Office Box 643328 Vero Beach, Florida 32964

Table of Contents

A Green Lunch

Do you know what a green lunch is?

No, it isn't green beans and broccoli!

A green lunch is a lunch that doesn't leave behind plastic wrapping, or other non-reusable packaging, that can end up in our **landfills**.

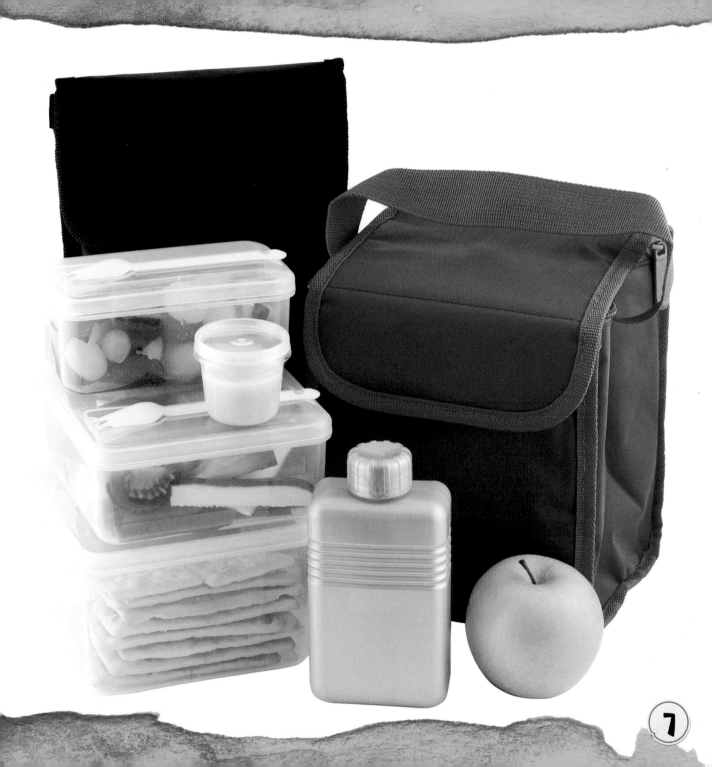

A green lunch is Earth friendly.

Bring It Green!

Some packaged drinks aren't Earth friendly.
The packages, or containers, are made
from plastic that can't be **recycled**.

Think Green!

It takes some packaging more than 100 years to **decompose***.*

You can be Earth friendly by packing **reusable** containers in your lunch.

A thermos is one kind of a reusable container you can use again and again.

Fruit, vegetables, and sandwiches that are packed in reusable containers are good choices for green lunches.

Can you think of other foods that would be a good choice for a green lunch?

Buy It Green!

Even if you buy your lunch at school, you can still have a green lunch.

Many schools have Earth friendly lunchrooms. A green lunchroom uses reusable dishes, cloth napkins, and silverware.

Green lunchrooms have recycle bins and **compost** bins.

Leftover food that is put into the compost bin decomposes and turns into plant food.

If your school doesn't have a green lunch program, you can help get one started.

Think Green!

Get Going with Green Lunches!

- Talk to your parents and
principal about green lunches.

- Make a poster that shows what
a green lunch looks like.

- Pack green lunches to show
your friends how easy it is to
be Earth friendly.

Green lunches are healthy for you and the Earth.

What's in your lunch today?

Mini-Landfill Experiment

What you will need:

- ☑ A plastic tub the size of a shoebox, or a gallon size Ziploc bag
- ☑ Loose soil
- ☑ A calendar
- ☑ Trash pieces such as a banana peel, apple core, a piece of bread, shredded paper, grass clippings, plastic wrap, a rubber band, a paper clip

What to do:

1. Fill the container 1/2 full with soil.
2. Mix in small pieces of trash from the list.
3. After you fill your container with some trash, dampen the soil with a small amount of water. Keep the soil moist but not muddy.
4. Place your mini-landfill in a sunny spot.
5. Mix your dirt every day.
6. Each day, record on the calendar what you are noticing about the trash.
7. After 30 days, empty the container onto a newspaper and spread out the trash.

What trash is decomposing?
What trash isn't decomposing? Could you recycle these things?

Glossary

compost (KOM-pohst): a mixture of rotted leaves, vegetables, fruit, etc., that is added to soil to make it richer

decompose (dee-kuhm-POZE): to rot or decay

landfills (LAND-filz): large areas where garbage is buried

recycled (ree-SYE-kuhld): to process old glass, plastic, and aluminum to make new products

reusable (ree-YOO-zuh-buhl): something that can be used again rather than be thrown away

Index

Websites

www.kidsbegreen.org

www.nationalgeographic.com

www.nwf.org/rrgreenzone

About the Author

Colleen Hord lives on a small farm with her husband, llamas, chickens and cats. She enjoys kayaking, camping, walking on the beach and reading to her grandchildren.